WOMEN OF SMOKE

MARJORIE AGOSIN

TRANSLATED BY

NAOMI LINDSTROM

LATIN AMERICAN LITERARY REVIEW PRESS
SERIES: DISCOVERIES
PITTSBURGH, PENNSYLVANIA

YVETTE E. MILLER, EDITOR

1988

The Latin American Literary Review Press publishes Latin American creative writing under the series title *Discoveries*, and critical works under the series title *Explorations*.

Originally published in Spanish by Ediciones Torremozas, Madrid 1987.

Library of Congress Cataloging-in-Publication Data

Agosin, Marjorie.
 Women of smoke.

 (Discoveries)
 Translation of: Mujeres de humo.
 I. Miller, Yvette E. II. Title. III. Series.
PQ8098.1.G6M813 1988 861 87-36203
ISBN 0-935480-34-X

Women Of Smoke can be ordered directly from the publisher:
 Latin American Literary Review Press
 2300 Palmer Street
 Pittsburgh, Pennsylvania 15218

Acknowledgements

This project is supported in part by grants from the National Endowment for the Arts in Washington D.C., a Federal Agency, the Commonwealth of Pennsylvania Council on the Arts, and Wellesley College.

The translation was funded in part by the Dallas TACA Centennial Fellowship in the Liberal Arts, University of Texas at Austin.

Cover and photograph by Paz Errázuriz, leading Chilean photographer and recipient of a Guggenheim Fellowship in 1986.

Table of Contents

Preface

Pierre Emmanuel, writing the Book *Saint-John Perse*, *Praise and Presence*, makes the confession: "To penetrate the work of a great poet requires an effort of renunciation. One should get away from his or her own personality and become another person, if that is possible. One should submit not only to a new rhythm, but also to the energy that produces it and makes it unique." Such is always the case when a writer of fiction, a poet, an essayist, sets out to comment upon a significant work by another author.

Marjorie Agosin has something special: she is extremely original in her subject matter and in the language in which she makes poetry out of it. The heroines of her voices are women and the environment that surrounds them is smoke, that gaseous product into which carbon particles are transformed to die: the voices of her women including Penelope, Ariadne, Diana, Virginia Woolf, Olga Orozco, Marta Traba, friends, compañeras, gypsies, lovers, prisoners, victims of rape, suicides, homeless and silent women, witches, beggars, loners, housewives, insomniacs, seem to stand out in their due perspective in the "narrations/ of/ women turned/ to smoke." What happens is that the smoke smothers them and immortalizes them till they become themselves through the power of a new language summoned up out of dreams, hyperbole, a long, hard look at pain and the vital force of pleasure, as well as through a determination to keep on changing the dominant ideological order because so much injustice cannot be possible. In Marjorie's poetic discourse there are no pitiful cries or hysterical accusations; there is a language of women who live and suffer, who love and whose stories unfold in the raw reality of smoke, a metaphor for their subjugation and the discrimination that plagues them.

Marjorie began her literary life in 1977 with the book *Chile: gemidos y cantares*. The famous novelist María Luisa Bombal wrote the foreword and called the author: "A poet already wise in her art at twenty-two years of youth. A prose writer as brilliant as she is sure-handed."

Luzmaría Jiménez Faro, the distinguished Spanish poet, introduced her in the original Spanish version of *Women of*

Smoke, saying: "Women under the lash, dressed in white, tender, torn, crystal pure, treacherous, sleepless, suicidal, in their burial shrouds. All of them holding hands with the Chilean writer Marjorie Agosin, whose deep concern with women's issues has been apparent in her various essays and articles." She added that since her first book, Marjorie Agosin has continued to develop flawlessly.

Marjorie was born in Bethesda, Maryland, in 1955, to Chilean parents. She has not lost her Spanish; she lives it, she thinks it, and writes it with precision and beauty. She received her doctorate at Indiana University and she teaches literature at Wellesley where the Spanish poet Jorge Guillén taught for twenty-five years.

She has published the following books of poetry besides this one *Chile: gemidos y cantares* (Santiago, 1977): *Conchalí* (New York, 1980), *Witches and Other Things* (Pittsburgh, 1984), and *Hogueras* (Santiago, 1986).

Her literary criticism includes: *Silencio e imaginación: metáforas de la escritura femenina* (Mexico, 1986) and *Pablo Neruda* (Boston, 1986).

With *Women of Smoke*, the reader will find in Marjorie a traveler who reaches all of Latin America, nothing and nobody escaping her profound and intelligent eyes. In Uxmal she encounters swallows, she hears the birds of Tulum, pisco brandy floods her memory, she runs into "shawls as red as firestone," she comes upon the "primeval poverty" of our cities, in Chile she wanders across gypsy women, in the Riviera Hotel she strikes camp for a moment to make "love like mixed-up ice," in Atitlán she discovers that "as a woman/ I have no country/ only stones/ and rivers,/ an illusion/ without citadels."

Marjorie also travels through history and encounters Ariadne, Diana, Penelope, the victims of Salem in 1692, Gabriela Mistral, Virginia Woolf on the afternoon when the river seduced her.

Marjorie has learned a great deal and now has this advice to offer:

Penelope
wife of sleepless nights,
don't weave a homecoming

because nobody today
comes home from
Ithaca.

Or she gathers centuries of experience into the last stanza of
"Salem":

My body was
a spreading fan
a waft of stones and roses.
They saw I was no
witch
I was
a woman
visible invisible
amid that smoke.

As in "Woman Hanged," she recognizes that

and her body joined the seaspray
of the voiceless women,
of those who obey
someone else's hands.

In "The Suicide," written with Gabriela Mistral in mind and
her poem "Tú me miras y me vuelvo hermosa," there is an
esthetic metaphysics concerning the right to life and the right to
death:

She the suicide
burning among the stones,
Under the water
making night into
a secret
and life into
nothing
more
than
a woman stretched out among the stones burning
her sound heard

in our absence,
I look at her
looking more and more beautiful.

The traveler Marjorie gives us an image of reality and utopia
in the world of women in her poem "First Birth."

They insisted she should,
had to open those legs
open them until she brought forth madness
and little bloody prisoners
punctured bruises
scraping at her cavities
They made her open up her legs
so life could pass through her extremities
Delirious, numb after so much pain and so much fear,
tied to that indelible pain of life.
And she obeyed, never to obey again.

Marjorie is a traveler, a traveler with deep, sensitive eyes.
Her collection of poems *Women of Smoke* is also a traveler,
now published in a bilingual edition. It will reach many
readers, and each one of them will attest to the accuracy of its
insights. As in olden times, each reader will discover that the
clearest profiles and the most faithfully rendered voices come
out of smoke.

Carmen Naranjo

Mujeres de humo

El viento reinando sobre
estos territorios,
azotando el contorno de los
vendavales,
el viento feroz, delirante asomándose
por las ventanas rasuradas
del miedo,
oyéndome en cada
vértigo de mis dolores,
sujetándome mientras me
trizo de frío
y este viento amarrándome como bozal o mordaza
haciéndome cada vez más segura
prisionera
en un páramo abandonado
en las embalsamadas
historias
de las
mujeres
de humo.

Women of Smoke

The wind, reigning over
these domains,
lashing the storm struck
countryside
the savage wind, demented, peering
out from windowpanes
shorn away in fear
sounding out my every
dizzy swerve of suffering
holds me pinioned till I
shatter in the cold
and this wind, these muzzling swathes,
bind me ever faster
a prisoner
on a godforsaken plain
with herb-preserved
narrations
of women turned
to smoke.

Ella

Como una herida a la intemperie,
despojada en la plenitud
de la piedra,
o el silencio de la
memoria,
Ella sabe que estorba.
Que no se encuentra
Que es una luz extranjera,
una sílaba
relegada
a los juegos de
la tiniebla.

She

Like a wound left out in wind and rain
ravaged in the fullness
of the stone,
or the soundless space of
memory,
She knows she's in the way,
and at loose ends,
an alien light
a syllable
cast off
to the games of
darkness.

La amortajada

El la besa en ese cuerpo que se estira y escapa por la redondez de sus pechos de agua, por la extensión de sus uñas de plumas.
El la besa como en una pesadilla que adormece.

The Shrouded Woman

He kisses her on that body that stretches out and escapes round
the curve of her breasts of water, down the length of her
fingernails of plumage.
He kisses her as in a nightmare that
can lull to sleep.

Uxmal

En Uxmal su cabeza ardía, plasmada de golondrinas
y antiguas memorias rescatadas.
Cuando la miraban y se miraba,
salieron pájaros poblados
en las dulces mieles de sus orejas.
Sus cabellos de sustancias cobrizas
se llenaron de travesías
y su boca alucinada era un lienzo de sol
errante en la celebración
de las golondrinas.

Uxmal

In Uxmal her head was afire, a mass of swallows
and old dredged-up memories.
When they looked at her and she at herself,
birds came forth, thronged
in the sweet honeys of her ears.
Her hair, made of coppery stuff,
was full of journeys
and her delirious mouth was a kerchief of sun
wandering in the celebration
of the swallows.

La pajarera

Se detiene
ante la
sepultura
de los pájaros
mientras asombrada y
amanecida
los oye
volar
entre sus
encierros.

The Bird Vendor

She stands
at the
graveside
of the birds
as astonished and
awakened
she hears them
fly
in their captivity.

Marinas

Yo sueño soñando entre las mareas hondas,
perversas de la demencia.
Sueño costras desvistiéndose de mi piel.
Sueño trozos desnudos de sol y tiempo.
Sueño que soy un eclipse mal parido
hasta que tú me desvelas
me abres y crecen del florecido soñado cabello,
espasmos azules, peces que regresan a mis ojos,
aguas que comienzan
a desmayarse.

El cuerpo como las olas obsesionadas en su sincronía,
pide nacer entre las caricias
y se hace un solo abrazo
soñado desde el brazo de tu sueño.
soñándose desde el fondo del mar.

Seagoings

I dream dreaming into deep-piled tides
grown perverse in their dementia.
I dream encrusted peelings working my skin free
I dream naked chunks of sun and time
I dream of being an eclipse, aborted
till you rip away my veil
open me and from the flowering dreamed out hair,
fits of blue, fish homing inwards to my eyes,
water edging to
a swoon.

The body, like waves obsessively in synch,
asks to be born with a caress
becomes one vast embrace
dreamed out from the arm of your dream
dreaming into being from the bottom of the sea.

Vidrios

Crispada, rencorosa, medita sobre sus botellas azules.
Sobre la luz del aire y de la muerte.
Y una mano golpea en el
cobalto prodigioso de los vidrios.

Crispada es un acorde de presagios y gestos desconocidos.
Ensimismada, poblada de ecos, recorta los vidrios
entre sus manos y goza del carmesí derramado.
Se imagina ser una antigua navegante por las heridas
desmemoriadas y descuartizadas.

Se detiene en un trozo de carmesí,
lo devora asustada,
palpa una y otra vez las adormecidas heridas
y todas sus caricias
se vuelven una sola mirada
en el azul cobalto de sus
botellas azules.

Glass

Clenched and spiteful, she ponders over her blueglass bottles.
Over the light of air and death.
And a hand slams into
the prodigious cobalt of that glass.

She's clenched into a chord of omens and unfamiliar gestures.
Self-absorbed and harboring a set of echoes, she cuts the glass
against her hands and savors that spilt crimson.
She sees herself in ancient times, a woman sailing down
amnesiac, disarticulated wounds.

She pauses over one red sliver.
In terror, she
devours it.
She runs her fingers over and over the sleeping wounds
and every stroke
coalesces to a wholeness gazing out
from the cobalt blueness of her
blueglass bottles.

Meditación ante un espejo

Me mira,
temerosa le devuelvo
obsequios, un trozo de piedad.
Límpiame me dice,
y los coágulos rosas flotan
salvajes por sus pechos
heridos de cruces negras.

Límpiame,
sáname de estas heridas soberbias
nos abrazamos,
le sujeto las yemas desprendidas,
le beso sus heridas
le prometo regresos.

Ella me mira
y me desata
mis manos.

Meditation in a Mirror

She looks at me;
fearfully I offer her
gifts in return, a piece of pity.
Wipe me clean, she tells me
and the pink clots float
savagely across her breasts
wounded by black crosses.

Wipe me clean,
heal me of these haughty wounds
we hold each other
I press her loosened fingertips back into place
I kiss her wounds
I promise to be back.

She looks at me
and frees
my hands.

Ante el espejo una mujer se peina los cabellos

Cuando se peina o se pinta,
se alza como un pez
y sus cabellos se envuelven
se revuelven
en el peine de la
abundancia.

Ella mientras se peina
es una fiesta de rojizos
coloridos,
un arpa de madejas encendidas
se imagina paisajes:
una bailarina desfigurada con su danzante matorral de cabellos.
Una madre recién nacida robándole fecundas miradas al espejo
seco.
Una desaparecida apareciendo entre las yerbas grises.
Una garza embrujada.

Cuando ella se peina
crecen rescoldos
y hebras bendecidas.

A Woman Combs Her Hair Before the Mirror

When she combs her hair or makes her face up,
she rises like a fish
and her hair entwines
entangles
in the comb of
abundance.

As she combs her hair, she
is a festival of brilliant
shades of red
a harp of weaves aglow
she imagines scenes:
A disfigured dancer with her dancing underbrush of hair.
A newborn mother stealing fecund glances from the dried-up
mirror.
A disappeared woman appearing among the gray weeds.
A heron fallen under a spell.

When she combs her hair
embers grow
and blessed strands.

Arreglos florales

Para Isabel Cámara

Eligió oficios de hacedora.
Talló constante y precisa
un ataúd radiante, delgado,
una bóveda de pandoras y porcelanas.

En ella, desmenuzó hojas blancas,
nada más que flores secas,
emboscadas de azucenas
restos de los velorios
de un amor
rasgándose en la
doble trampa de
esas flores secas.

Floral Arrangements

for Isabel Cámara

She chose to be a maker of things.
She carved away, constant and precise,
at a slender, glowing coffin
a vault of pandoras and fine china.

In which she pieced apart white leaves
nothing but dried flowers
ambushes of lilies
remainders of the wake conducted
for a love
left scratching at itself,
dually entrapped among
those dried-out flowers.

El amor y la calavera

Tiene miedo a ser arrastrada como presa desfigurada.
Tiene miedo a ese instante donde la vida es un tablero
de damas movedizo.
Tiene miedo a una guitarra viuda mofándose de sus silencios.
Tiene miedo del amor y de sus quejas pero se deja que
él la cubra de golpes dislocados, suaves
enfermizos como en un bosque de cloroformo.

Tiene miedo,
pero deja
que la besen.

Love and the Death's Head

She fears being dragged off like a mutilated prisoner.
She fears that moment when life becomes a shifting
checkerboard.
She fears a widowed guitar laughing at her silences.
She fears love and its discontents, but doesn't stop him raining
blows upon her, soft,
unhealthy as a forest grown of cloroform.

She fears,
but lets
them kiss her.

Amas de casa

Sentía ese miedo inquietante
ante el cuerpo de los pájaros muertos
que una mano pasajera
depositaba junto al sofá de brocado.
Encogida
escrutinaba las horas,
y a esas extrañas aves
reposando en sus muebles de caoba.

Ociosa se inventaba oficios.
Recortaba papelitos
y abría espantada las puertas
que se cerraban una y otra vez
recordándole a la música
de huesos y clarividencias.

Quería jugar a la vida.
Se perfumaba en ese paisaje de las aves recostadas
entonces, jugaba con ellas.
Divagaba junto a las escobas,
hablaba con las viejas muñecas de porcelana cancerosa.
Jugaba, reía,
era una ama de casa
limpiando la sangre entre los muebles de caoba
y un sofá de brocado.

Housewives

She felt that troubling fear
at the bodies of dead birds
that a passing hand
left lying there beside the brocade sofa.
Shuddering
she eyed the time,
and those unknown birds
resting in mahogany boxes.

Idly she invented tasks.
She cut out scraps of paper
and fearfully she opened doors
that always closed back up
to remind her of the music
of bones and premonitions.

She hoped to play the game of life.
She perfumed herself against the backdrop of recumbent birds,
then she played a game with them.
She rambled off amid the brooms,
conversed with ancient dolls of cancerous china.
She played, she laughed
she was a housewife
wiping clean the blood between mahogany boxes
and a brocade sofa.

Insomnia

Déjate ya de oscuridades,
de esos mutilados orificios
que acechan cabelleras
insomniadas.
Ven,
acércate y apaga con tu
rostro los temores,
esas figuras inútiles
que nos acechan
ante la planicie
de las sábanas
y las enconadas maderas
de la
habitación.
Apaga esas luces
para que la
piel, como una arena dormida
entre
los fuegos
nos alumbre
nos haga descansar
de los rostros que
se acercan.
Apaga esa
luz
apágala.

Insomnia

Give up your darknesses,
those mutilated orifices
lying in wait for sleepless
heads of hair.
Come,
come closer, let your face
subdue the fears
those useless figures
lurking in ambush
across the flat expanse
of bedclothes
and the spiteful
wooden stretches
of the
room.
Turn out those lights
let skin,
like sleeping sand
among
the fires,
become our light
and offer us relief
from the looming
faces.
Turn out that
light
out
out.

Iluminada

Entra sin temblores.
Segura de sus actos.
Atraviesa corredores
y sacude la ratonera.

Lleva dos cirios en
sus espléndidas y pérfidas manos
de niña larga.
Acarrea sus huesos pesadísimos,
livianos,
como pájaro, buitre o gaviota.

Recoge el vaso de vino,
el felino la contempla
y sabe...

Acarrea sus huesos
camina en una monotonía
incesante
sin navajas ni
escapularios
comienza ese dulce final
pero antes,
ilumina
su casa
para que la
vean
deslumbrante,
pálida,
muerta,
iluminada.

Woman Aglow

She strides in unwavering.
Sure of her moves.
She takes the hallways
shaking out the mice.

She bears two candles in
her splendid, faithless hands
like a lanky woman child.
She bears along her heavy bones
as light
as a bird, vulture or seagull.

She takes the wineglass
the feline studies her,
he knows...

She bears along her bones
striding onward in ceaseless
monotony
no knives, no
scapularies
she comes to that sweet dénouement
but first
she sets her house
alight
to let them
see her
dazzling,
drained of color,
dead,
aglow.

La condenada

Antes de la hora de morir,
elige rosadas flores,
silvestres cadencias
rosadas
como su pubis
que resueña cabizbajo,
afixiándose en
ese cuerpo sin
sentido,
en ese cuerpo
atravesado por
inutilidades y destinos.

Antes de la hora
de una tregua,
se viste de
esas rosadas flores
se adorna sus caderas,
se ciñe toda
de rosado
y un gran silencio
la declara
la reina del
pubis
huérfano.

Woman Sentenced to Death

Before it's time to die,
she gathers her pink flowers
wild-blooming cadences
pink
as her pubis
resounding upended,
suffocating in
that body with
no meaning,
in that body
shot clean through with
senselessness and fate.

But it's time
for a reprieve,
she adorns herself
with those pink flowers
embellishes her thighs
enfolds herself
in pink
and a mighty silence
acclaims her
queen
of the orphan
pubis.

A Laura Riesco

Peligrosamente,
como por un desfiladero,
entramos olvidadizas, rajadas
a conversar con la Amparo
junto al viejo mantel de hule,
al agua flotando y recién salida
de las hierbas.
Intercambiamos regímenes
entre madejas y lunas
noticias de difuntas y paridas
bajo el chiflido de vientos andinos
de cocinas espolvoreadas entre la grasa.

El pisco corre por la memoria
de una nostalgia que tal vez,
nunca fue nuestra
en un agujero de nación
que nos enseñó
correctamente
a contar constelaciones, instituciones, hijos.

Peligrosamente
regresamos
para llamarnos por los espejos
soy yo la Amparo,
la Eloísa,
cargando casas en el pelo
soy yo doña Marina
a sabiendas
como el eco
que ya
no
somos
las   mismas
las

mismas.

To Laura Riesco

Dangerously,
like snaking through a mountain pass
we come drifting in forgetfully
to sit and talk with old Amparo,
the ancient oilcloth stretched across the table,
the water floating fresh
from off the herbs.
We talk of diets
here among the skeins of yarn and looking glasses,
who's died, who's had a child,
set against the whistling of the wind from off the Andes
of kitchens splotched with grease.

Pisco floods the memory
drenching with nostalgia times that, like as not,
were never really ours
in a native hole
where they taught us
one right way
to count up constellations, institutions, offspring.

Dangerously
we come back
to call upon our mirror selves.
I am Amparo,
Heloise,
bearing houses in my hair.
I am Doña Marina
and know I am
like the echo
that we now
no longer
are
those   same girls
those

girls.

La mendiga

A Raquel en la esquina de Plaza Vergara

Era una presencia segura
jamás amenazadora
y siempre familiar,
mientras extendía sus manos inclinadas
por el crujido del hambre.
Mientras lentamente abría sus yemas,
sus dedos que olían a los estiércoles
de inservibles abanicos.

La veían reposada,
recostada entre el azar de una pobreza
inquietante
mientras su mirada, era una arena ardiente
sumida en el silencio locuaz de los transeúntes
que avergonzados
ejercían la caridad diurna.

Y entre las pesadillas de una ausencia milenaria,
la mendiga se cubría con chales rojizos como los pedregales
con chales violetas como la paz de los muertos,
o los sueños de los heridos.
Sus chales deslumbraban,
eran trozos de idiomas y legados secretos.
Eran vaporosos,
como las damas que después del ocio
y la oscuridad acarician prendas.

La veían con esa mano extendida
cabizbajos paseaban los visitantes temporales de las aceras
y ella sólo veía sus envolturas de chales llenos de hebras y
    piedad.
Y yo la veía en las zonas flotantes de sus tapados.

The Beggar Woman

To Raquel at the corner of Plaza Vergara

She was just supposed to be there,
never threatening,
always familiar,
outstretching hands weighed down
with creaking hunger
as she slowly spread her fingertips
her fingers smelling of the offal
of broken fans.

They'd see her in repose,
at rest against the troubling poverty
life dealt her
while her eyes sank burning sand
into the talky silence of the passers-by
who shamefacedly
performed their good deed for the day.

And shrouded in nightmares of a thousand years' absence
the beggar woman wrapped herself in shawls as red as firestone
in shawls as purple as the peace of the dead,
or the dreams of the wounded.
Her shawls were dazzling
shards of secret languages and legacies
wispy
as the ladies who, in idle
darkness, stroke their finery.

They'd see her with that outstretched hand
those who only used the sidewalk to pass by cast down their
    eyes
and all she saw were her encircling shawls, full of loose threads
    and pity.
And I saw her in the unmoored spaces of her wrappings.

Sola

Inventada
interrumpida por extrañas vegetaciones
escucho depurada rituales extraños,
manos languidecidas tocándose,
oigo a veces chirridos errantes
donde nada me pertenece
ni el aliento del tiempo
o la hierba humedecida tras
las marejadas.

Soy enfermizamente ajena
cerrándome en los
umbrales
buscando la familiaridad
de ciertos gestos,
o los olores del patio
de mi abuelo.

En el despertar,
apartada de las leñas,
sola entre las
dunas,
son palabras extranjeras
que me interrumpen
que me callan
que no me dicen.

Alone

A pretend woman,
cut off by unknown growths
scoured and drained, I listen to unfathomed rituals,
languid hands in contact
at moments all I catch are whirring jangles
with nothing there for me
not the breath of time
not the grasses dampened
by retreating tides.

I am morbidly alone
clamming up in every
doorway
eager for the old familiar touch
of certain gestures,
or the home smell
of my grandpa's courtyard.

Awakening
far from hearthwood,
alone among the
dunes,
foreign words come round to
interrupt me
silence me
never
tell me.

La reina

Se declaró
reina
a sabiendas que su
trono
era un banco de paja
habitado en las
destartaladas
plazuelas de
una ciudad
sin voz.

Sus atuendos
eran chales apestados
por la cotidiana
presencia
de una pobreza
atávica.

En vez de
corona,
llevaba extraños
eucaliptus ingenuamente
desordenados por
su cabellera de piojos.

Su cetro,
una vara
de árbol desconocido,
moribundo.

Pero ella era
una reina
las aves participaban de su rito
y las extrañas mujeres vestidas de blanco que
la cuidaban
también.

Se declaró reina.

The Queue

She hailed herself
queen
knowing full well that her
throne
was a wicker parkbench
taken in the
rundown
little plazas
of a city
with no voice.

Her raiment
shawls befouled
by the daily presence
of primeval
poverty.

For a
crown,
she wore odd
eucalyptus straggles, crudely
mingled through
her flea nest hair.

For a scepter,
a cropping
of some unknown,
dying tree.

But she was
a queen
the birds observed her rite
and the unfamiliar women dressed in white who
cared for her
did too.

She hailed herself queen.

En Chile, en las Gitanas

Las gitanas, habituales,
crepitando en la nebulosa del escamoteado silencio,
son astutas itinerantes,
son las brujas del palpar
que en el azar,
de las sombras y los almendrales
me acechan
para ceremoniosamente cortarme mi mano,
y la guardan en las alas doradas de su áridos vestidos,
alucinados se trastornan en una madeja de hilos dormidos
y mi mano extendida sujeta residuos,
historias de este cuento de las desdentadas.

Me dicen:
Por tu buena voluntad
déjame verte la suerte,
déjame inventarte monedas,
despójate de espejismos ilusos
acércate, nómbrame, convídame tu lengua.

Mi mano anochece,
ellas dicen:
es el azar,
y las demenciales gitanas transcurren
acarreando mi mano
que ahora es espejo carmesí
marcando las huellas de sus peregrinaciones.

In Chile, Gypsy Women

The gypsy women, now habitual,
rustling in the nebula of silence spirited away,
they're clever transients,
witches feeling out the way.
In shifting fates
of shadows and of almond groves
they lie in wait for me
to ritually excise my hand
and stash it in the golden wingspread of their arid garb;
delirious, they tangle in a skein of sleeping strands
and my outstretched hand tamps down the dregs,
stories of this tale of toothless women.

They tell me:
come on,
let me look into your future,
let me coin new coins for you
come free of your illusions
come closer, name me, share with me your tongue.

Night comes over my hand.
They say:
that's fate
and madmaking gypsy women flow along
bearing off my hand
now a crimson mirror
marking off the traces of its wanderings.

Mujeres fábulas y yo

Me decían,
verde verdita
verdosa verdimia
verde que te quiero
más verde
y viva Lorca en las palabras.

Le decían
vendimia
por sus ojos como pozos
frondosos, deliciosos
deshojando delicias
de parras iluminadas
en la oscura cripta
de su boca aún
no verde.

Y eran verdes sus manos
como los árboles
Y eran verdes sus yemas
mientras separaba hierbas, oréganos, dientes de ajo y cilantro.
Y eran verdes sus palabras
mientras preparaba ceremoniosa
la savia de las plantas
y recortaba una divina alcachofa.

Sus muslos
olían a verdores
como ventisqueros y bosques
y eran verdes sus secretos
como el musgo aterciopelado
de sus viviendas.

Verdes eran sus sabidurías,
sus palabras
mientras desenterraba su
verdad
en una verdosa fragancia.

Women of Legend and I

They called me
missie greenjeans
green, green, you're a bean
green I love you green
grown greener
and Lorca forever in the word.

They called her
the great green queen
for her eyes like wellsprings
ferned out free, delicious
leafing loose delights
of glowing grapevines
in the darkened crypt
of your mouth still
not gone green.

And her hands were green
as trees
and her fingertips were green
as she sorted herbs, oregano, cloves of garlic, coriander.
And her words were green
as she ritually prepared
the herb-milk
and carved a sacred artichoke.

Her thighs
smelled of greenery
as if wafted from the woodlands
and her secrets were green
like the velvet moss
of her abodes.

Her wisdom was green
her words
while she unearthed her
truth
in a greenful fragrance.

Ariadna

Ariadna, Ariadna, Diana, ellas marcan caminos como tú. En
    sus manos
llevan hilos tapizados alrededor de angostas cinturas.

Ariadna es una
viajera.
Juega contorneándose encima del agua que la acaricia y la
    siente.
De sus piernas nacen hilos
y algas adormecidas.
Todo florece en ellas, de ellas todo florece.

Hoy borda, sueña y escribe árboles. Sus dedos son los colores
    guardados
en la orilla de sus labios. Ariadna eres tú cuando ríes y cuando
lloras.

Ariadna supo cuidarlo-quererlo entre las cavidades del mar.
Él la amarró como una roca anciana.
Mientras lo quería
él la anudó de los hilos que florecían del desflorecido pelo.

Ariadna valiente
construyó una nave de sus
cabellos
y él en la nave de Ariadna
se fue silbando entre las mares.

Ariadna en Naxos supo de las ausencias,
mientras que con las hebras de Ariadna,
él, más lejos que las orillas,
él, navegante astuto y solitario.

Ariadne

Ariadne, Ariadne, Diana, they made their way like you. In their
    hands
they carry strands, worked in close to gird the slender waists.

Ariadne is a
woman in transit.
She plays a game of turnings as the water from beneath caresses
    her and feels her.
From her legs
strands and sleeping seaweed
issue forth.
Everything flowers in them, from them, everything flowers.

Today she plies her needle, dreams, writes trees. Her
    fingers are the colors
that she keeps beside her lips. Ariadne is you, when you
    laugh and when you
cry.

Ariadne managed to care for him, to love him in the hollows of
    the sea.
He bound her round like an ancient rock.
As she loved him,
he worked her into knots with the strands that flowered from
    her deflowered hair.

Dauntless Ariadne
built a ship out of her
hair
and in Ariadne's ship
he whistled off across the seas.

Ariadne in Naxos learned about absence
while with Ariadne's strands
there he was, beyond the shores,
the clever, solitary sailor.

Ariadna aprende de las esperas y de tu ausencia
y llora por el dolor del olvido, del abandono,
y los hilos de antes la ahorcan en la tierra.

El navega solitario
navega por un sargaso
por las manos de Ariadna. Ariadna, Diana
que ahora extraviadas en las arenas flotan
como esqueletos de humo.

Ariadna llora.
Ariadna ríe
Ariadna eres tú.

Ariadne learns from waiting and from missing you
and weeps the pain of one forgotten and abandoned
and her longtime strands now strangle her on land.

He sails on, solitary,
sails through floes of gulfweed
through Ariadne's hands. Ariadne, Diana
now drifting loose across the sands
like skeletons of smoke.

Ariadne weeps
Ariadne laughs
Ariadne is you.

Penélope II

Penélope,
¿hacia dónde vas
con ese cabello vencido,
desembocando por el mar?
la mar,
donde Ulises escucha y se desata
en el mugir de las sirenas antiguas
que entre vientos y delirios,
le cubren de caricias
los pies,
de hombre infiel a las esperas
y tú
Penélope,
destejiendo una mentira,
cruzándote de
alas,
de piernas,
cóncava guardando una noche de amor entre los huecos palillos
de tus manos,
Penélope,
esposa del insomnio
no tejas regresos
porque hoy nadie
vuelve de
Itaca.

Penelope II

Penelope,
where are you going
with that defeated hair
flowing out into the sea?
The sea,
where Ulysses listens and works loose his bonds
at the moaning of the ancient sirens
who, in a whirlwind of delirium,
enfold his feet
in their caresses–
a man unfaithful to the years of waiting
and you
Penelope
unraveling a lie
crossing your
wings,
your legs,
concave, still harboring one night of love in the hollows of your
hands,
Penelope,
wife of sleepless nights
don't weave a homecoming
because nobody today
comes home from
Ithaca.

Hechicerías

Enrojecida por el rebozo rojizo de sus amores,
alucinada por el vestido rojizo de sus visiones,
se sube al carruaje blanquecino.
Otra vez tiene que huir de las emboscadas
de las travesías de dolor.
Y su cuerpo es una arruga entre las oscuridades.

Los iracundos de la aldea la persiguen
y cubren de sábanas blancas sus pisadas.
Pero ella adivina sus zapatos.
En la aldea,
con velas de cuero negro la persiguen
y se exhala en la nocturna niebla
de los que la temen.

Witchcraft

Reddened with the reddish shawl of all her loves,
delirious with the reddish shawl of all her visions,
she crawls aboard the bleached-out wagon.
Once again, she had to flee the wiles
of lurking pain.
And her body is a wrinkle in the dark.

The wrathful townfolk come for her,
muffling footsteps in white bedclothes.
But she can tell their shoes.
In the village they
go after her with candles of black leather
and she's breathed out in the nighttime mist
of those who fear her.

Salem

En la jadeante y triste
luz de Salem,
junto a las ramas que arden
como emblemas nefastos,
en ese encorvado año
de la hora oculta: 1692.
Devoraron las entrañas
de mi mantilla fosforecente,
verde como los sueños de
Irlanda.

Me rajaron
en una torre
mi cabellera indomable,
bondadosa.

El más pérfido
cortó mis orejas
y los sonidos del
agua le apagaron
la sed de sus manos mancas.

Me acusaron de envenenar
tortas, dulces, pasteles,
cuando yo jamás fui
cocinera,
sólo acumulaba hierbas para
sanar alegrías y espasmos.

Fui cristalizada
con mis manuscritos y conjuros
mis débiles posesiones,
el candelabro
de mi abuela.

Salem

In the sad and gasping
light of Salem,
where branches burn
like signs of things turned bad,
in this huddled year
of the hidden time: 1692.
They left it gutted,
my phosphorescent shawl,
green as dreams of
Ireland.

In a tower,
they left me shorn
of my stubborn
goodhearted hair.

The lowest of them all
cut off my ears
and the sounds of
water slaked
the thirst in his wanting hands.

They claimed I poisoned
pastries, cakes, and sweets,
but I was never
any cook,
I only gathered herbs to
soothe commotions or the fits.

I was crystallized
with my manuscripts and spells
my frail belongings,
my grandma's
candle-tree.

Los generosos de la aldea,
las casandras blancas,
gemían, ahullaban,
mientras yo era una madeja
de humo,
una mujer de humo,
danzando inválida
por las hogueras.

Después de muerta
nací:
en el vientre
del mar
o tal vez del
mismo fuego.

Mis huesos brillaron en las noches
de medias lunas,
practicaba las ceremonias
de mejorías
desde las profundidades
subterráneas de mi agua.

Mi cuerpo
era un abanico,
una fragancia de rosas y estrellas.
Supieron que no era una
bruja,
era
una mujer invisible-visible
tras las rendijas
del humo.

The charitable goodmen of the town,
the white Cassandras,
moaned, shrieked,
while I became a tangled skein
of smoke,
a woman made of smoke,
dancing crippled
through the bonfires.

After dying, I was
born:
in the belly of the sea
or perhaps
out of the very fire.

My bones gleamed when
the moon was half full,
I practiced healing
rites
from my
water depths
beneath the earth.

My body was
a spreading fan
a waft of stars and roses.
They saw I was no
witch,
I was
a woman
visible-invisible
amid
that smoke.

Perdida

Herida transcurre, es una perdida en los páramos insaciables.
Dice que anda en busca de su cabaña, ruca o tienda.
Quiere adormecer su cuello de gacela,
su rostro hundido replegándose ante un líquido enfermizo.

El sendero detiene su marcha lenta.
Nadie la deja obedecer al dulce mandato de sus pies livianos
el sendero inventa una memoria extraña.
La detienen los pájaros, las fisuras de las rocas.

Herida busca un país,
sus ríos
los patios habitados.

Herida dicen que la recogieron
mientras su muñeca desprendida
caminaba hacia los páramos.

Lost Woman

She travels wounded, a woman lost on the insatiable plains.
She says she's looking for her cabin, hut or tent.
She wants to cradle her gazelle-like neck,
her sunken face recoiling from a sickly liquid.

The path shuts off its slow progression.
No one lets her heed the sweet urge of her light feet
the path invents a strange remembrance.
Birds stop her, and the cracks in the rocks.

Wounded, she seeks a country
its rivers
the lived-in patios.

Wounded, that's how they say they took her
while her doll, broken loose,
walked onward toward the plains.

Recordar

Recordar no era peligroso,
porque en el silencio
ella podía ser una
bóveda abierta,
una selva benigna para
inventar.
Y ella recordaba la luz atravesando su cuerpo desnudo frente a
    un
trozo
azul de tiempo.
Recordaba las palabras que su boca, como el humo, iba
    trazando
en los paseos y murmullos por una ciudad sin mar.

Cuanto le gustaba recordar,
la monótona travesía por
la playa
o las sombras de arena que
seguían sus huellas.
Ella, recordaba el rumbo
incierto de las mareas
y entre las horas, pronunciaba
el movimiento de las olas,
los besos contra el roquerío
todo, para poder recordar: llamar-amar-escribir.

En sus inmensos cuadernos, entre sus dedos,
ella memorizaba aquellos nombres de
todos los días,
aquellos mansos transeúntes
que desaparecieron
pero no de su recuerdo,
porque ella llamaba, gritaba y
sus delgadas manos escribían
el mensaje en los papiros,
en las botellas azules
que navegaban no a una deriva.

Remembering

Remembering wasn't dangerous,
because in silence
she could be an
open vault,
a friendly jungle
to invent.
And she remembered light slicing through her naked body
    facing a
blue
swath of time
And she remembered the words that her mouth, like smoke,
    traced out
in the strolls and murmurs through a landlocked city.

How she liked remembering,
the monotonous trip across
the beach
or the shadows of sand that
followed her tracks.
She remembered the uncertain
way the tides went
and, between times, she'd pronounce
the movement of the waves,
the kisses up against the rock
everything, just to remember: calling-loving-writing.

In her vast notebooks, on her fingers,
she memorized those names
like any others,
those gentle passers-by
who disappeared
but not out of her memory,
because she called and cried aloud and
her thin hands wrote
the message on papyrus,
in the blue bottles
sailing, not adrift.

Ella recordaba sus
viajes
por la piel antigua
del que la abandonó por la manía del olvido,
y ella lo pensaba,
mandándole hebras doradas que se desprendían de la redondez
de un sueño,
soñado tantas veces
sólo para nombrarlo
soñándolo
sólo para
soñarlo
nombrándolo.

She remembered her
journeys
across the ancient skin
of the one who left her for sheer love of oblivion,
and she thought him up,
sending him golden strands that reeled out from the roundness
of a dream
dreamt so many times
only to name him
by dreaming him
only to
dream him
by naming him.

Mudas

Desequilibrada,
anunciaba otras palabras,
impedía que se confundieran con las ya dichas.
Era una trapecista de sus idiomas
porque pedía hablar
en medio de un
ahuecado silencio.

La muda es una viciosa, mira el agua, la
    luz
acercándose
en el espejo del sol iracundo.
De su boca, se desprenden babas malolientes.
Todos la temen,
todas se mofan de sus ojos quejándose a borbotones.
La muda mira el contorno de un paisaje tapizado de
    sonidos
y su boca es una perversa sequía.

Silent Women

Unbalanced,
she bespoke fresh words to come,
she kept them separate from those already said.
She was a flying acrobat of languages
because she asked to speak
amid a
hollow silence.

The silent woman is degenerate, she looks at the water, the
    light
drawing near
in the mirror of the angry sun.
Foul-smelling spittle dribbles from her mouth.
All the men fear her,
all the women laugh at her eyes overflowing with moaning.
The silent woman looks around at a landscape coated with
    sounds
and her mouth is a perverse stretch of drought.

Vagabundas

No la inquietan sus posesiones
y deambula encrispada,
ensomniada por
las aceras, por los rescoldos del
frío,
Nadie la espera
ella a nadie aguarda
y en su bolsa bordada por los agujeros
del humo
guarda hojas secas
azucenas y terrores
guarda una sábana enjaulada
para los insomnios
y trozos de huesos
para reposar
su cuerpo
navegado, vaciado,
y acusador.

Afuera, duermen los
protegidos,
los techos los resguardan
toman agua, la luz los mece y adormece
pero ella al filo de las
ventanas
en las trizaduras del aire
se desparrama
como una guardiana nocturna
y se deja estar
embrujada, dolorosa
porque nadie la espera
y ella a nadie espera.

Homeless Women

She gives no thought to her belongings
and walks on, drawn in,
sleepless, down
the sidewalks, over live cinders of
cold.
No one expects her
she expects no one
and in her bag adorned with holes
of smoke
she keeps dry leaves
lilies and terrors
she keeps a sheet imprisoned
for the sleepless nights
and bits of bones
to rest
her body
criss-crossed, emptied-out,
accusing.

Outside, they sleep
protected,
roofs hover over them,
they have a drink of water, light lulls and cradles them
but she, at the windows's
edge
in the shards of air
scatters wide
like a night watchman
lets herself fall
beneath a grievous spell
because no one expects her
and she expects no one.

La ahorcada

Parece que la ahorcan,
que la arrastran
por peregrinaciones escarpadas,
que alguien la acecha
mientras
canta o muere
y con habilidad
de mago o vidente
le acaricia el cuello
con astucia,
hasta con amor.
Ella no sabe si se
está acercando a las
tumbas
desoladas de sus abuelas,
o si en esas manos ensombrecidas,
que con destreza la buscan,
se acerca a una vida peligrosa
más allá de sus deseos
más allá de sus días.

Parece que la ahorcan
y su pelo se trastorna en una
ola adormecida
y su cuerpo se une a la espuma
de las sin voces,
de las que obedecen
a unas manos ajenas.

The Woman Hanged

It seems they hang her,
they drag her
down steep pilgrimages,
someone lies in ambush
as she
sings or dies
and with the skill
of a magic-worker or a seer
strokes her neck
with cunning,
even with love.
She doesn't know whether she's
nearing the desolate
graves
of her grandmothers,
or whether in those shadowed hands,
that seek her out expertly,
she's nearing a dangerous life
beyond her desires
beyond her days.

It seems they hang her
and her hair tumbles wild in a
sleeping wave
and her body joins the seaspray
of the voiceless women,
of those who obey
someone else's hands.

Escrito pensando en Gabriela Mistral y su poema, "Tú me miras y me vuelvo hermosa".

La Suicida

Entre las piedras,
desnuda entre los vestigios
con la boca entre dormida
y abierta
con los brazos apresurados
por el des-amor
ella
se vuelve hermosa
mientras la vemos
simple, extinguida
como la noche misma
ella
la suicida
que surge ante los transeúntes
en una inmensa plenitud
en una pregunta mentirosa
por qué
sangra en su vestido de escamas
¿por qué tiene olor a muerte
y a culebras destrenzadas?

¿Por qué se fue?

Ella nos mira
y cada vez se vuelve más hermosa
porque es ajena y
descendiendo en un círculo
alrededor de
sus manos que no desean
de su piel con fragancias y
crisantemos
de su pelo como una historia
de caricias nunca ciertas.

Written while thinking of Gabriela Mistral and her poem "You Look at Me and I Grow Beautiful."

The Suicide

Among the stones,
naked among the vestiges
with her mouth half asleep
half open
her arms driven
by lovelessness
she
grows beautiful
as we look on
simple, gone out
like night itself
she
the suicide
there for the world to see
in a vast fulfilment
in a liar's question
why does
she bleed into her coat of scales
why does she smell of death
and unraveled snakes?

Why did she go away?

She looks at us
growing more and more beautiful
because she's elsewhere and
descending in a circle
around
her hands that want nothing
her skin with fragrance and
crysanthemums
her hair like a story
of never-true caresses.

Ella la suicida
ardiendo entre las piedras.
Sumergida entre las aguas
haciendo de la noche
un secreto
y de la vida
nada
más
que
una mujer extendida entre las piedras ardiendo
oyéndose
en nuestra
ausencia.
Yo la miro
Y es cada visión más hermosa.

She the suicide
burning among the stones.
Under the water
making night into
a secret
and life into
nothing
more
than
a woman stretched out among the stones burning
her sound heard
in our
absence.
I look at her
looking more and more beautiful.

Virginia

Sabía que más que el vivir,
la muerte supondría ciertas
preparaciones:
un bastón para los ancianos incautos
una inmensa piedra robada de
la tierra,
y el río,
para hundirse.

Virginia

She knew that more than living,
death would call for certain
preparations:
a cane for the reckless elderly
an immense stone stolen from
the earth,
and the river,
to drown in.

Primer parto

Le insistían que debía
que tenía que abrir esas piernas,
abrirlas hasta extraer locuras
y pequeñas presas ensangrentadas
moretones triturados
rajando sus cavidades.
Le obligaban a abrirse de piernas
para que pasara la vida por sus extremidades.
Delirantes, adormecidas de tanto dolor y tanto espanto,
amarradas a ese dolor imborrable de la vida.
Y ella obedecía para después nunca más obedecer.

First Birth

They insisted that she should,
had to open up those legs
open them until she brought forth madness
and little bloody prisoners
punctured bruises
scraping at her cavities.
They made her open up her legs
so life could pass through her extremities.
Delirious, numb after so much pain and so much fear,
tied to that indelible pain of life.
And she obeyed, never to obey again.

Día de playa

El sol y la ausencia rodeándola.
Lamiéndola,
El sol como un suave cuchillo recorriéndola,
haciéndola brillar con languidez.
Devolviéndole una piel diáfana, diurna.

Ella no evade la caricia,
se deja que la quieran
porque a veces la han oscurecido obligándola a hincarse.
Porque a veces la han poblado de pájaros chamusqueados
y silenciosas visiones.

Y ahora ella con el sol atado,
como un carrusel de tricolores sonidos.
Y ella abriéndose ante la claridad,
se desata de su traje de mustia señora efímera.
Y es una luz la que la traspasa y baña.

El placer es un trozo de seda ardiente
frente a las madejas abrazadoras de sus manos.

Cierra los ojos,
suele verse desvestida en la periferia de la playa,
se confunde con los eclipses de madera.
Al mar, nada pide
sólo aprende de la paciencia de un sol que la asombra.

Goza vertiginosamente por su propia espalda
entre una vigilia o un sueño.
El sol vela por la espalda inclinada.
Ella por fin quiere ser feliz
y los cuchillos rodando por sus pies
son ahora raíces benignas.
Todo por el sol que la vela en una duermevela.

A Day at the Beach

Sunlight and absence all around her.
Licking her.
The sun like a smooth knife slithering over her,
setting her agleam with languor.
Giving her back a translucent, daylight skin.

She doesn't shrink from that embrace,
she lets them love her
for there were times they dimmed her and forced her to her
    knees.
For there were times they mobbed her with scorched birds
and silent visions.

And here she is now, with the sun in tow
like a carrousel of three-colored sounds.
Here she is now, opening to the glow,
free of the trappings of a faded, tenuous lady,
and it's a light that cuts clean through and bathes her.

Pleasure is a swatch of burning silk
to her hands' embracing skeins.

She closes her eyes,
often sees herself naked at the beach's edge,
mingling in among the wooden eclipses.
She asks nothing of the sea,
learns only from the patience of a sun that leaves her dazzled.

She pleasures dizzily in her own back,
mixing waking into dream time.
The sun stands guard as she lolls back.
She tries, at last, for happiness,
the knives at her feet
now harmless roots.
It's all the sun
that holds the drowsy woman in its care.

Moteles

Sórdidos, agujereados por la ausencia,
éramos rojizos silvestres
y nos arropábamos en las sábanas de la inmundicia.
Riviera Hotel,
era esa pieza oscura donde ausentes e imprecisos
disfrutábamos del maligno olor a papas fritas
y nauseabundas cervezas derrotadas.

Eramos dos solitarios
plasmados de humo y espejos extranjeros.
Esperábamos brisas propicias
un tiempo mejor para olvidar
el Rivi era Hotel
y el amor como un hielo trastocado.

Motels

Sordid, riddled with absence,
we were wild savages
and wrapped ourselves in sheets of sleaze.
Riviera Hotel,
was that dark room where, absent and imprecise,
we savored the vile smell of fries
and nauseous defeated beers.

We were two loners
made of smoke and foreign mirrors.
We were waiting for the right winds
better weather to forget
the Riviera Hotel
and love like mixed-up ice.

El jardín de las delicias

Ellos se aman en
el parque
vertiginosamente
se deslizan
sobre yerbas
y amapolas.
Alguien les dice
que son impúdicos
otros cuerdos ancianos
complacidos celebran
los cabellos confusos
entrebesándose por
los matorrales.

Un niño juega
a perseguir una
mariposa,
se atropella
ante su paso
dulce y torpe.
La mariposa y el niño
se ríen
porque ninguno es capturado.

Los soldados pintados
asustadizos y cobardes
espían a los que juegan en los parques
piensan que se confundirán con las grandes
encinas,
con las grandes murallas de amarillos
pero ellos no saben, no pueden saber
que los que se aman, que los niños
inclusive esa mariposa,
también los ven.

The Garden of Delights

They love each other in
the park
dizzily
they slither on
the grass
and poppies.
Someone tells them
they're indecent
other saner old folks
are pleased to see
their heads of hair entangled
exchanging kisses in
the underbrush.

A child plays
at catching a
butterfly
takes a tumble
following its sweet and clumsy
moves.
Butterfly and child
both laugh
since neither one gets caught.

The painted soldiers
jumpy and craven
spy on whoever plays in the parks
they think they'll blend in against the
giant elms,
against the massy rows of tamarisk
but they don't know, they can't know
that those who love each other, that the children
even that butterfly
see them too.

Diciembre

Primera nieve del año,
alucinada
mirándome,
con su rostro de bruja ingrata
y ese invasor silencio.

La blancura destemplada,
como un rostro que huye
gravita.

Dime, tú tienes miedo
mientras el despellejado, calvo,
nos hace
señas de pavor entre las pisadas?

Nieves del año,
augurios,
de las presencias,
de las ausencias
en una
memoria.

Y alguien allá,
se desliza
como un alfabeto
escribiendo los
nombres de
la nieve,
de la poesía.

December

The year's first snow
delirious
looking at me
with a face like a thankless witch
and that intrusive silence.

The overload of whiteness
like a fleeing face
bears down.

Tell me, does it scare you
when the flayed-bare bald man
signals fear
among the footsteps?

This year's snows,
auguring
the presences
the absences
in a
memory.

And someone there comes
slipping round
like an alphabet
writing the
names of
the snow,
of poetry.

Desnudez

A Milan Kundera

Le aterraba esa desnuda uniformidad
que exigía el despojo, lento
preciso de las prendas
rayadas y
grises
como los sueños de la guerra.

Tenía miedo
a que le dijesen
desnúdate
enséñame tus senos
rasurados,
cortados por la
grieta calva
de los miedosos.

Tenía miedo
a esa desnudez
frente a los
espejos uniformados
de sus padres
que al mirarla
engendraban
oscuridades oscurísimas.

Le aterraba esa desnuda uniformidad
en un país
visitado por los otros.

Nakedness

to Milan Kundera

She was terrified of that naked uniformity
that meant being stripped, slowly
and precisely, of her striped
gray
clothes
like dreams of war.

She was afraid
they'd tell her
take your clothes off
show me your breasts,
shaven,
slit with the
bald incision
you see on people
who are scared.

She was scared
of that nakedness
in front of
mirrors wearing uniforms
her parents'
who when they looked at her
brought on
darkest darknesses.

She was terrified of that naked uniformity
in a country
frequented by others.

Aquel hombre que me hizo escribir mi primer

Libro de amor,
prefería la enfermiza
seguridad
de la cama bien
tendida
sin menses,
sin sémenes
adormecidos.

Quería la ropa
albísima
para poder untarse
de vicios.

Prefería el
beso cotidiano
que no muerde,
que no hiere.

Quería niños
en su lugar
y muñecas inmóviles.

Prefería esa seguridad
ante la ilusión
desbordada
de una mujer
de humo
con zapatos
rojos
y un inmenso
sombrero
morado.

That Man Who Made Me Write My First

Book of love,
preferred the sickly
safety
of the well-made
bed,
no menses,
no semen
sleeping there.

He wanted his clothes
purest white
the better to besmirch himself
with vices.

He preferred the
routine kiss
that never bites
that never wounds.

He wanted children
in their place
and stock-still dolls.

He favored that security
over the rampant
fantasy
of a woman
of smoke
with red
shoes
and a huge
purple
hat.

Los países del humo

Mi país
es el aire tan
nuestro
en las noches fugitivas
de Atitlán.

Es tu rostro
vendado,
aunque salvajemente
hermoso
a pesar de esos
movimientos
entorpecidos
por las ajenas cuchillas
afiebradas.

Y tú
despojada
abierta
herida
eres
iluminada
un faro en
los mares del sur.

Mi país
son los gemidos
del hambre,
en la africana noche atrevida
suplicante para que no la olvides.

Como mujer
no tengo
país
tan sólo piedras
y ríos,
una ilusión
sin citadelas.

The Lands of Smoke

My country
is the air so
much our own
in the fugitive nights
of Atitlán.

It's your blindfold
face,
still savagely
beautiful
despite those
movements
hampered
by the
strange and fevered
knives.

And you
ravaged
open
wounded
are
aglow
a lighthouse in
the southern seas.

My country is
the moans
of hunger
in the African night, boldly
imploring you not to forget her.

As a woman
I have no
country
only stones
and rivers,
an illusion
without citadels.

908 - 2725832

Nena (Rosby).